Tax Lien Properties California Real Estate Tax Lien Investing for Beginners

How to Find & Finance Tax Lien & Tax Deed Sales

By

Greene E. Blank

Table of Contents

Chapter 1 State of California Overview

Chapter 2 How To Purchase Investment Property

Chapter 3 Tax Sale Property Overview

Chapter 4 REAL ESTATE FINANCING 4,000 Sources!

Chapter 5 Find California Wholesale Real Estate Fast!

Chapter 6 California Real Estate Investing City Goldmines

Chapter 7 Goldmine of Government Grants

Chapter 8 Business Insurance

Chapter 9 Millionaire Real Estate Investing Rolodex

Chapter 10 Real Estate Investing Terms

Chapter 1

State of California Overview

State of California Overview

It's reported that California got it's name from a romance novel. In the early 16th century Author Garci Rodriguez de Montalvo wrote the romance novel "Las Sergas de Esplandian"...The Adventures of Esplandian. In the book was a mythical island named California populated by only Black Amazon warriors who used only gold for weapons and tools.

One of the things that makes California a great place to be a real estate investor is that the population has 39.6 million residents. The highest state population in the United States!

The California median household income is $71,805. That is the 9th highest in the United States.

Other interesting facts about California:

Spoken languages: English: 58.1%, Spanish: 28.9%, Chinese: 3.0%, Filipino: 2.2%, Other: 7.9%

Motto: Eureka

State song: "I Love You, California"

State Nickname: The Golden State

State Capital: Sacramento

Biggest city: Los Angeles

Area: 163,696 square miles

State of California Overview

Any business person, especially a real estate investor, wants to have a business where the customer base has plenty of money. Another thing that makes California a fantastic place to be an investor is it's $3.0 trillion dollar economy. It is the largest in the United States! If California was a country, it would be the 5th largest economy in the world. More great invesor numbers...In 2017, California's San Francisco bay per capita personal income was $94,000.

The 2019 unemployment rate in California was 4.3 percent, compared to the United States national average of 3.8 percent.

The economy in California is quite diverse. 58 percent of the state's economy revolves around real estate services, technology, scientific, government, technical, business services and finance. The Agriculture industry in California, has the largest output in the United States.

The California economy has the 5th highest gross domestic product in the world at $2.7 trillion dollars, surpassing the United Kingdom.

State of California Overview

Points of interest in California

Yosemite National Park. Sequoia National Park, San Simeo State Park and Point Reyes National Seashore. California has 278 state parks and beaches.

Disneyland Park, originally Disneyland, is the first of two theme parks built at the Disneyland Resort in Anaheim, California, opened on July 17, 1955. Recently, Disney reported a record annual profit of $12.6 billion on $59.43 billion in revenue.

The Golden Gate Bridge. The Golden Gate Bridge is a one mile wide suspension bridge that connects San Francisco Bay and the Pacific Ocean.

Hollywood. Also known as Tinseltown, has tourist landmarks like the Chinese Theatre, Dolby Theatre, Paramount Pictures and is home of the Academy Awards...the Oscars.

Billionaires in California

California has the largest number of billionaires in the United States. 124 billionaires call the state of California home. They have a net worth of over $532 billion dollars.

So there is plenty of money to be made in California and it is your job as an investor, to make sure as much as possible finds it's way to your bank account.

Chapter 2

How To Purchase Investment Property

Expert Strategies to Purchase Property

Expert Strategies to Purchase Property

AVOIDING & MANAGING & ELIMINATING RISK

Legendary Real Estate investor Dave Del Dotto once said "stick with the government, they will make you rich.". Real Estate is one of the safest investments in the world, when done properly. There is risk just driving to the grocery store. The only thing separating you from a head on collision is a yellow strip of paint. That being said, there are risks in every financial investment decision you make.

Do your research. Know what you want to do, before you begin. Are you looking to flip properties? Hold on and make money on the interest rates? Are you looking for a property to live in? Are you looking to rent out properties? Each decision requires a different type of research. If you are looking to rent out properties then you need to research what the local apartment complexes and homes are renting for in the area. If you are looking to flip a property then you need to find a real estate agent that can give you comps that have sole in the area within the past year.

Visit any property you are going to purchase. You do not want to get stuck with swampland or a unbuildable lot.

Expert Strategies to Purchase Property

AVOIDING & MANAGING & ELIMINATING RISK

You also don't want to get stuck with a property that has high property taxes. Learn the property tax rates of all the counties in the state that you are going to invest in.

Make sure that the property has not been condemned.

Make sure that the property does not have numerous costly violations of city codes.

Ask multiple real estate agents for information on any area you are interested in investing.

Ask about possible environmental issues.

Research possible liens by builders and contractors.

Beware of a owner who may declare bankruptcy on a property. This is a manageable risk but because laws change constantly, consult a real estate attorney for more information on how to handle this risk.

Avoid scams by dealing with government employees as much as possible.

Expert Strategies to Purchase Property

1. Decide how much you can afford to invest and stick with the numbers you come up with. Avoid something called Auction fever. It can be started by a "fast hammer". A fast hammer is when the auctioneer closes the auction early at a amazing price. It is designed to get your attention and get a fever about being the next one in the room to get a "Great Deal". When you go to a auction you should have a list of properties you have research and what your bid is going to be. This will help you to avoid Auction Fever.

2. Research. Single family homes with at least 3 bedrooms are great investments if purchased at the right price. Your research tells you what the right price is. Remember to use real estate agents and their access to the multiple listing service. Also many big companies like Remax and Century 21 have websites up with tons of information on the real estate area you wish to invest in.

www.trulia.com

www.zillow.com

www.biggerpockets.com

https://www.census.gov/quickfacts/table/PST045216/00

http://www.realtor.org

Those are just a few of the great sites to get research information on real estate.

Expert Strategies to Purchase Property

3. Get in contact with local counties for a list of delinquent properties for sale. Also ask when the sales will take place. Ask if you can be put on a mailing list. Use the internet to track down as much information as you can. Don't be afraid to use search engines other than Google. Bing and Yahoo are also great search engines to use.

4. Buy from other investors. Some people get in over their head. As long as you know the numbers and have research the property, it does not matter who you purchase it from as long as it is a good deal. One investor in Michigan recently purchased every single property for sale at a tax auction. He has to sell those properties or he is responsible for paying the taxes. As Carelton Sheets once said "you can't rationalize murder" so how can you rationalize why someone might offer you a great deal? Just do your due diligence on the property before making a deal.

5. Establish a relationship with local officials. Learn the names of the people who work in government offices that will be giving you information. Visit in person and say thank you. Call and say thank you. Send them a card that says thank you. How many people do you think do that for them? They will remember you. I worked for the government for over 20 years. I still remember the woman who repeatedly gave me lemon-aid when it was hot outside.

Expert Strategies to Purchase Property

6. Buy early in the Year. When you buy a tax lien certificate, back taxes have to be paid to the treasurer as well as interest and penalties. Redeem the property and you could be earning interest on this larger amount of money. If the property is not redeemed you can turn in the tax lien certificate and be handed a deed for the property, any extra amount you pay for the certificate comes from you because you could have gotten the same property for less.

7. Try smaller counties you may have much less competition.

8. Invest in your comfort zone. Try to find mentors who have already done what it is you want to do. As your knowledge and experience increases then you can take on bigger projects.

9. Write down your goals. Remember to answer the question of why you are doing this in the first place. A powerful why will keep you motivated when it comes time to do the legwork required to be successful.

10. Take Action. There are plenty of smart people who are poor. Proper Knowledge plus action is the key to success.

Expert Strategies to Purchase Property

In microeconomics total cost (TC) describes the total economic cost of production and is made up of variable costs, which vary according to the quantity of a good produced and include inputs such as labor and raw materials, plus fixed costs.

In English... you factor in as many external costs, not just the cost of the investment property.

In order to be successful when buying investment property, you have to be good at determining the Total Cost of a property.

11. Get Investment Property Market Value

Wholesale Real Estate is real estate that is real estate priced under it's retail value. But how do you know that the retail value of real estate property? The standard formula for finding the value of real estate is to have a real estate agent find comparable (comps) properties that have sold recently. Usually about 4 properties with in a mile of the purchase property, that have sold within the past year. Formulas vary from bank to bank and real estate agent to real estate agent.

Today you can get a rough estimate by doing the research yourself. Remember that a bank will probably use their own formula, but at least you can try to get a ball park figure of a properties value by using these web sites.

Expert Strategies to Purchase Property

Appraisal Web Sites

https://www.zillow.com/how-much-is-my-home-worth/

http://www.eppraisal.com/

12. Selecting a Real Estate Agent

So now that you have found a property, researched it's value, it's time to make an offer. Some times you have to use a government approved agent to make an offer. Like any profession, there are good agents and not so good agents.

When I lived in Virginia, once a year the local paper published a list of all the top real estate agents for almost every real estate agent franchise/business. If your local paper does not do that then here is a formula I use for selecting a real estate agent.

Expert Strategies to Purchase Property

No part timers. Part time effort usually gets you part time results. I want an agent whose livelihood depends on their success.

Size Does Matter

The size that matters. The size or amount of properties sold. Not necessarily the gross amount of property value sold. Suppose you had a real estate agent who sold 1 million dollars worth of real estate and another who sold $500,000 worth of real estate. Which one do you choose? It depends. I want the agent who has sold the most individual properties, and not necessary the one who has the highest gross. An agent can sell only 1 house for a million dollars. The agent who sold $500,000 worth of real estate may have sold 10 $50,000 homes.

Usually a agent who makes a lot of sales has a good marketing formula in place and a good team of agents working with or for her/him. Don't be afraid to ask "who's your best agent? Why?". Often a real estate company will try to toss their worst agent a bone. Don't be that bone. Remember they work for you. Their commission comes from the property you are investing in.

Some courses teach you to negotiate the commission. I believe a proficient agent is worth the commission they desire. It's your job to select a proficient agent.

Expert Strategies to Purchase Property

13. "100-3" Formula

Here is a quick and easy formula for getting a great deal on a real estate investment property, using a real estate agent that you have build up some rapport with.

Have the agent find 100 properties for sale that have been on the market for at least 90 days. Have the agent fax an offer of 25% below market value to all of the properties. Because the properties have been on the market for at least 90 days, you are dealing with motivated sellers. It is likely that 10 out of the 100 will accept your offer. Now filter through the 10 and select the best 3 properties. Use these filters to help you select the best 3.

Strategies To Making Offers

1. What are the property taxes?

2. Are there any Homeowner Association dues?

3. What will be the appreciation value?

4. What will be your utility expenses.

5. How much will it cost, to be "live-in" ready.

6. Is it the lowest valued house in the neighboorhood?

7. What is the Crime Rate

Expert Strategies to Purchase Property

Property Taxes

I once owned two homes free and clear. The homes were in the same state. Both were similar in size, but one had a $3,000 a year property tax and the other one was $300 a year in property taxes. You can guess which one I moved first. Property taxes are often overlooked, but can be a big factor in the (TC) total cost. Do your research before you make an offer.

HOA (Home Owner Association)

Usually when a house seems like the perfect deal, but has been sitting on the market for a long time, look to see what the HOA dues are. Personally I stay away from any property that has HOA dues, because they can escalate and you have no control over them.

Appreciation

Look at the history of real estate appreciation. It can vary greatly form city to city, and neighborhood to neighborhood. If you are going for a quick flip then this is not that important.

Utility Expenses

The importance of the expense depends on what you are going to do with the property.

Expert Strategies to Purchase Property

Rehab Expenses

If you are not an expert, have a professional inspect the house so you can factor in, a accurate estimate of rehab expenses. Be aware of any possible code violations as well.

Cost relative to the Neighborhood

Usually it's easiest to sell the cheapest house in the most expensive neighborhood. However if you just plan on renting the house then this is not as big a factor.

Crime Rate

The crime rate can have a big impact on resale value. Use web sites like https://www.crimereports.com/ to help understand it's impact on your property.

Expert Strategies to Purchase Property

14. "Take what the defense gives you"

Take what the defense gives you is a sports metaphor for viewing the landscape of a situation and adapting to what you see.

Take a similar approach to making offers in real estate. If you tell a "For Sale By Owner" everything that is wrong with the house he or she spend a lifetime building... you may insult the owner and lose the deal.

However, you send a list of needed repairs to a HUD representative, he may reduce the price of the property, no questions asked.

Adjust your offer making strategy to the person or organization you are dealing with. The farther removed a person is from the property, the less emotional they are about making deals.

Know your profit numbers and stick to them. Especially if you are bidding on a property. Be aware of Auction fever. It will bring out the competitive nature in you and can lead to you over bidding on a property. Know your numbers and be disciplined. The reason you pick out 3 properties in the 100-3 formula is so that you have 2 other properties to go to, if your first choice does not work out.

Chapter 3

Tax Sale Property Overview

Tax Sale Property Overview

Buying Tax Lien and Tax Deed Properties

What are Government Property Tax Sales?

A government property tax sale is a public auction that the government uses to recover delinquent real estate property taxes.

Why does the county have the public auction?

If a propety owner can not pay the delinquent taxes, the public auction gives the county the oppurtunity to recoup the back taxes owned, and recover any penalties and interest due. It puts a sense of urgency on the property owner and gives those that have the money to pay the taxes an opportunity to get a property at a discounted rate.

Tax Sale Property Overview

What is a Internet public auction tax sale?

By using the internet to hold a public auction, counties are able to have bids placed using a computer, and widen the potential number of buyers.

Who can participate in the online public auctions?

Anyone who registers and then places a pre-bid deposit can participate in online auctions.

What is a Tax Deed?

A tax deed is a document used to show title to real estate after the property has been sold at a public auction, by the government in charge of collecting property taxes.

Tax Sale Property Overview

What is a tax deed public auction sale?

A tax deed sale is a public auciton for property that has a tax default. The deeds to the property are sold to the highest bidder. Usually the bidding starts at a combination of the penalty fees, interest charges and the delinquent taxes.

Tax Deed states are:

- Alaska
- Arkansas
- California
- Connecticut
- Delaware
- Florida
- Georgia
- Hawaii
- Idaho
- Kansas

Tax Sale Property Overview

Maine

Michigan

Missouri

Nevada

New Hampshire

New Mexico

New York

North Carolina

North Dakota

Ohio

Oklahoma

Oregon

Pennsylvania

Rhode Island

South Dakota

Tennessee

Texas

Utah

Tax Sale Property Overview

Virginia

Washington

Wisconsin

What is a Tax Lien Sale?

A tax lien sale is a public auction authorized by the state government for tax liens of real property. Tax liens are sold for the amount of a combination of the penalty fees, interest charges and the delinquent taxes. You do not own the house when you purchase a tax lien. You own the right to get paid all of your money back, with interest after a set time period that varies with each state. The interest rate also varies with each state.

Tax Sale Property Overview

List of Tax Lien Certificate States:

Alabama

Arizona

Colorado

Florida

Illinois

Iowa

Indiana

Kentucky

Louisiana

Maryland

Massachusetts

Mississippi

Montana

Nebraska

New Jersey

New York

Tax Sale Property Overview

Ohio

South Carolina

Vermont

Washington DC

West Virginia

Wyoming

Tax Sale Property Overview

Locate Nationwide Tax Sale & Foreclosure Auction Properties

http://www.bid4assets.com

Bid4assets is an amazing web site for quickly finding investment property. The landing page has a map of the United States and you can just move your mouse pointer over the state you are interested in to see if they have any property in their database.

Here are just a few of the assets you can target on this site!

* County Tax Sales

* Bank Owned Property

* US Marshal

* Real Estate

* Coins

* $1 No Reserve Homes

Tax Sale Property Overview

Locate Nationwide Tax Sale & Foreclosure Auction Properties

https://www.foreclosure.com/tax_lien_sales.html

Foreclosure.com is another great web site for instant access to property information.

Once on the landing page links to all the top cites for tax lien sales appear.

There is also a map of the United States and you just click on the state you are interested in.

The landing page also includes a nice summary of tax lien sales as well as links to:

* Hot Foreclosure Deals

* Cheap Homes (under 60K)

* Rent to own homes

This is truly an amazing web site packed with plenty of great deals for the serious real estate investor!

Tax Sale Property Overview

Government Foreclosure Properties

One advantage purchasing from the government is that there is no emotional attachment to the property. Don't be afraid to make a offer that is lower than the listed price. I once argued with a real estate agent who refused to place a offer lower than the stated price. Eventually I got him to place the offer. (Remember that they work for you, however some government properties can't be purchased unless you go through a HUD or government approved agent.) It was countered twice, before I decided to purchase another property. But they countered with two offers lower than the listed price.

If you are reading a ebook version of this book then you should be able to access these web sites by clicking the links below. But if you are reading a paperback version of this book then be careful when looking for government properties. There are many web sites pretending to be government web sites and some will attempt to charge you fees for information about government properties.

Tax Sale Property Overview

Government Foreclosure Properties

Fannie Mae
The Federal National Mortgage Association

https://www.fanniemae.com/singlefamily/reo-vendors

Department of Housing and Urban Development

https://www.hudhomestore.com/Home/Index.aspx

The Federal Deposit Insurance Corporation

https://www.fdic.gov/buying/owned/

The **United States Department of Agriculture**

https://properties.sc.egov.usda.gov/resales/index.jsp

United States Marshals

https://www.usmarshals.gov/assets/sales.htm#real_estate

Tax Sale Property Overview

Commercial Real Estate Properties

City Feet

is a nationwide database of Commercial Real Estate Property

http://www.cityfeet.com/#

The Commercial Real Estate Listing Service

is a nationwide database of Commercial Real Estate Property

https://www.cimls.com/

Land . Net

is a nationwide database of land, commercial real estate for sale and for lease.

http://www.land.net/

Loop . Net

is a nationwide database of Commercial Real Estate Property

http://www.loopnet.com/

Tax Sale Property Overview

Finally let's look at the incredible interest rates that tax property can give you.

Interest Rates & Redemption Periods

STATE	INTEREST	REDEMPTION	COUNTIES
ALABAMA	12%	3 YEARS	67
ARIZONA	16%	3 YEARS	15
COLORADO		3 YEARS	64
FLORIDA	18%	2 YEARS	67
GEORGIA	10%	1 YEAR	159
ILLINOIS	18% UP	2 ½ YEARS	102
INDIANA	10%-25%	1 YEAR	92
IOWA	24%	1 ¾ YEARS	99
KY	2%	3 YEARS	120
LOUISIANA	17%	3 YEARS	64
MARYLAND	VARIES	2-6 MONTHS	23
MASS	16%	2 ½ YEARS	14

Tax Sale Property Overview

Interest Rates & Redemption Periods

STATE	INTEREST	REDEMPTION	COUNTIES
MISS	18%	2 YEARS	82
MISSOURI	10%	1 YEAR	114
NEBRASKA	14%	3 YEARS	93
NH	18%	2 YEARS	10
NJ	18%	2 YEARS	21
NEW YORK	14%	2 YEARS	62
OKLAHOMA	8%	2 YEARS	77
SC	8%-12%	1-1 ½ YEARS	46
VERMONT	12%	1 YEAR	14
WV	12%	17 MONTHS	55
WYOMING	18%	4 YEARS	23

TOTAL COUNTIES   1,483

Tax lien and Tax deed property sales are a great way for an investor to either earn interest on their money or to get a property for pennies on the dollar.

CHAPTER 4

REAL ESTATE FINANCING 4,000 Sources!

8 Realistic Ways to Finance Real Estate

FINANCING REAL ESTATE

Welcome to Expert financing. I am going to show you several realistic ways to finance real estate. You are going to learn how to finance real estate with.

* VA LOANS

* PARTNERS

* INVESTMENT CLUBS

* CREDIT CARDS

* CORPORATE CREDIT

* EQUITY

* SELLER FINANCE

* HARD MONEY LENDERS

* AND FINALLY I SHOW YOU THE MONEY$!!

USING A VA LOAN

According to the web sites www.benefits.va.gov and www.military.com the current VA Loan amount is a whopping $417,000! What a lot of veterans don't know is that you can use that money to purchase not only your home, but investment properties. That is how I started my investing career. Purchasing multiple homes using my VA Loan.

FINANCING REAL ESTATE

Even if you are not a veteran, you can still partner up with one, who still has some money left on his or her VA LOAN.

If you are a Veteran, you will need to obtain a copy of your DD 214 and VA Form 26-1880 Request for a Certificate of Eligibility.

PARTNERS

This is another way I purchased a home. At the time I worked for the United States Postal Service. I had already purchased plenty of homes, so many of the workers were aware I had successfully invested in real estate. At break time I went around and ask people to partner up with me. I had multiple people offer to go in as a partner. I choose one and that house we rehabbed and flipped just two months after purchasing it. To this day it was the biggest gross profit on one deal, I have had. True I had to split it with my partner, but I would rather have half of something than all of nothing.

Having the combined resources of two people can be a great benefit, but it is not without it's challenges. If you are going to use a partner, no matter how close you are...GET EVERY THING IN WRITING.

FINANCING REAL ESTATE

Having a partner can dramatically increase the chance of a Bank lending money as well as having someone to split the work on rehabbing, should you decide to save money and make repairs yourself. But all this must be spelled out BEFORE you enter into a Agreement/Contract and purchase a home.

It helps if the person is like minded and understands the risks and benefits of investing, and truly understands the return on investment of a particular deal.

REAL ESTATE INVESTMENT CLUBS

Real estate investment clubs are groups that meet locally and allow investors and other professionals to network and learn. They can provide extremely useful information for both the novice and expert real estate investor. A top real estate club can provide a great forum to network, learn about reputable contractors, brokers, realtors, lawyers, accountants and other professionals. On the other hand, there are many real estate clubs designed to sell you. They bring in "gurus" who sell either on stage or at the back of the room, and as a result, the clubs typically profit to the tune of %50 of the sale price of the product, bootcamp, or training that is pitched.

FINANCING REAL ESTATE

I have purchased a ton of real estate books and real estate courses. Carlton Sheets, Dave Del Dotto, The Mylands, Seminar courses and much much more. I am not against any club bringing in a speaker who has a course. However I think there should be transparency to the members of the club.

There is certainly value in the networking that may come at one of these groups. But attend working to attain your goals and not necessarily the club's goal to sell you something. Some times both are the same thing. As a rule I usually leave debit cards at home the first time I attend an event. If there is a seller there with a "This day only offer" then I won't feel pressured to purchase. Plus most sellers can be convinced to sell at the discount offer price at a later time when you have had a chance to come down off the "sense of urgency emotional pitch" .

CREDIT CARDS

When using a credit card in real estate you must really do your homework on the deal. Dan Kennedy a world famous marketer once said "always stack the numbers in your favor". That's how you use a credit card. Look at the return on investment as compared to the long term cost of using a credit card and it's interest. Also I would recommend buying low cost homes that you can purchase and own free and clear.

FINANCING REAL ESTATE

No Mortgage Payment!!! My last 2 homes I have purchased have been cash deals. One home cost $1,500 and the other about $7,000. The first was a government property from HUD and the 2nd From a Bank. These institutions are unemotional about real estate and simply view a property as a non performing asset. The 2nd home was 4 bedrooms, 1 1/2 bath and a basement located in a farming community and came with a 2 car garage/shed and .6 acre(that is the size of a NFL football field) of land.

In this book I show you how to find plenty of houses with amazing below wholesale prices and a formula for almost always finding a great deal.

CORPORATE CREDIT

Many people set up corporations to buy and sell real estate as an additional protection against liabilities. Other's create a corporation to mask personal involvement in property transfers and public records. Regardless of the use of a corporation, you can buy real estate with corporate credit as an alternative to using your own cash or IRA. By capitalizing on the credit rating of your corporation, you can buy real estate and build your corporate holdings portfolio.

FINANCING REAL ESTATE

Just remember that you can set up your corporation in a state that favors you the most for your real estate deals. Do your research. Most people like Delaware and Nevada, but you will have to decide if your home state or any other state is best for you and your business.

CURRENT EQUITY

Using the equity in your home for real estate investing is another way you can finance properties. You might use the money for a down payment or it may only be enough to cover the cost of some rehab repairs.

If you stick to the low cost home formula, you may have enough to purchase the entire house. A house is an investment that should appreciate in value as well as give a great ROI (Return On Investment). When you decide to flip the property or rent it out for positive cashflow.

If you have equity and it's not doing anything, then you may decide to make it a "performing asset" and use it as part of your real estate finance program.

FINANCING REAL ESTATE

SELLER FINANCING

Seller finance is where the seller of a free and clear property becomes your bank along with being the seller.

Advantages:

You get to purchase the property on terms that may be more beneficial for you. Seller gets monthly payments and the benefit of treating the sale as an installment sale thus allowing them to defer any capital gains taxes that may be due.

Disadvantages:

You may be locked into a mortgage with a pre-payment penalty or may not be able to resell the property immediately. This strategy is typically not meant for flipping but can definitely be used for that purpose if structured correctly.

Seller Finance is a known way to finance a property. That is why I have presented it in this book. But it is my least favorite because you now have a lingering relationship with your property. Your ability to make decisions regarding the property is limited and for that reason, I would not go this route. However, like all types of financing, you have to ask yourself, "is the deal worth it."

FINANCING REAL ESTATE

I also prefer to work alone, but when a great deal came along, I sought out a partner to make it happen. Risk is usually relative to potential profit.

HARD MONEY LENDERS

A hard money lender is usually a individual or company that lends money for an investment secured by the investment property.

Advantages:

Less red tape to get the money. You are dealing with people who understand the real estate investment business.

Disadvantage:

This is not a long term loan. The lender wants a return on investment, usually within a few months, a a year, or a few years. The interest rate on the loan is much higher than usual conventional banks.

Using hard money has a higher risk because the return on investment is due quicker. Therefore it is a good idea not to use a Hard Money Lender, until you have a great deal of experience and confidence in being able to produce a return on investment.

SHOWING YOU THE MONEY

A list of web sites for financing.

www.businessfinance.com (4,000 sources of money!)

www.advanceamericaproperty.com

http://www.cashadvanceloan.com/

www.brookviewfinancial.com

www.commercialfundingcorp.com

www.dhlc.com
(hard money for the Texas area)

www.equity-funding.com

www.bankofamerica.com

www.carolinahardmoney.com
(for real estate investors in North and South Carolina)

www.fpfloans.com

FINANCING REAL ESTATE

As you can see there are plenty of strategies for financing a property. Do your research on your investment property and get the true market value. Purchase well below wholesale. This will help to minimize risk and elevate your potential profit margins. Buying below wholesale also creates a buffer for unexpected expenses.

So don't let the lack of money be a roadblock in your real estate investing dreams.

Chapter 5

California Cash Flow Counties of Wholesale Property!

California Cash Flow Counties of Wholesale Property!

The internet has made it possible to grow your real estate investing business quickly and easily. Now you can view hundreds of properties online without ever leaving your home.

In this chapter I am going to give you a ton of web sites and the addresses to government wholesale sources, to help you to cover this state's real estate goldmines. I have selected some of the biggest counties with the largest supply of wholesale real estate.

In general you should look at 100 homes for every 1 property that you purchase. Comparing factors like the home value, rent potential, repair cost, local taxes, possible home owner fees, utilities etc...

While there is no substitute for inspecting a home in person, having access to thousands of homes on the internet can help you to narrow down the field to spectacular deals! So take advantage of this knowledge to help secure your real estate investing success!

California Cash Flow Counties of Wholesale Property!

Locate Statewide California Properties

MLS.com

http://www.mls.com/search/California.mvc

California Real Estate Foreclosures with links to different cities on the landing page.

REALTOR.com

http://www.realtor.com/foreclosures/California

Links to California real estate properties by county and city.

Top California Counties

The previous web sites give you access to a broad selection of property in all the counties in California.

Next I narrow it down to a handful of the top counties based on the population size, rising property values, rental profit potential and the abundance of wholesale property available.

California Cash Flow Counties of Wholesale Property!

1. Los Angeles County

Los Angeles County has a population of 10,170,292 and is 4,060 square miles. In this county there are a large amount of Goldmine real estate investment oppurtunities.

Tax Property Info Street Address:

Los Angeles County Treasurer and Tax Collector

500 W. Temple St., Room 225, Los Angeles, CA 90012 Phone: (213) 974-2111 or (888) 807-2111

Foreclosures web Address:

https://www.realtor.com/foreclosures/Los-Angeles-County_CA

Tax Sales web site:

https://ttc.lacounty.gov/schedule-of-upcoming-auctions/

Auction and Sale of Tax-Defaulted Property

213.974.2045

auction@ttc.lacounty.gov

Find California Wholesale Real Estate Fast!

2. San Diego County

San Diego County has a population of 3,299,521 and is 4,204 square miles.

Tax Property Info Street Address:

San Diego County Treasurer and Tax Collector

1600 Pacific Hwy, Room 162, San Diego, CA 92101-2474   Phone: (877) 829-4732

Government property information :

Probate Property:

(858) 694-3500 or email Noel.Agarma@sdcounty.ca.gov

Surplus Property:

https://urlzs.com/R1CLc

Sheriff sales:

https://www.sdsheriff.net/courts/property-sales.html

Tax Sales web site:

https://urlzs.com/q4Qny

California Cash Flow Counties of Wholesale Property!

3. Orange County

Orange County has a population of 3,169,776 and is 790 square miles.

Tax Property Info Street Address:

Orange County Treasurer and Tax Collector

12 Civic Center Plaza, Bldg 12, Santa Ana 92701

Phone: (714) 834-3411

Foreclosures web Address:

https://urlzs.com/ubXKc

Tax Sales web site:

http://www.ttc.ocgov.com/proptax/pta/

California Cash Flow Counties of Wholesale Property!

4. Riverside County

Riverside County has a population of 2,361,026 and is 7,208 square miles.

Tax Property Info Street Address:

Riverside County Treasurer and Tax Collector

P.O. Box 12005, Riverside, CA 92502-2205

Phone: (951) 955-3900 Fax: (951) 955-3906

Foreclosures web Address:

https://urlzs.com/ogMzP

Tax Sales web site:

https://www.countytreasurer.org/TaxCollector/TaxSaleInformation.aspx

California Cash Flow Counties of Wholesale Property!

5. San Bernardino County

San Bernardino County has a population 2,128,133 and is 20,000 square miles.

Tax Property Info Street Address:

San Bernardino County Tax Collector

172 West Third Street, First Floor, San Bernardino, CA 92415-0360

Phone: (909) 387-8308

Foreclosures web Address:

https://urlzs.com/AzNAJ

Tax Sales web site:

https://urlzs.com/4ueXS

California Cash Flow Counties of Wholesale Property!

6. Santa Clara County

Santa Clara County has a population of 1,918,044 and is 1,291 square miles.

Tax Property Info Street Address:

Santa Clara County Tax Collector's Office

70 West Hedding Street, East Wing, 6th Floor, San Jose, CA 95110

Phone: (408) 808-7900

Sheriff's Sale:

https://urlzs.com/TqNRi

Tax Sales web site:

https://urlzs.com/JsMB8

Find California Wholesale Real Estate Fast!

7. Sacramento County

Sacramento County has a population of 1,501,335 and is 966 square miles.

Tax Property Info Street Address:

Sacramento County Department of Finance, Tax Collection Division

700 H Street, Room 1710, Sacramento, CA 95814

Phone: (916) 874-6622

Government Real Property:

https://urlzs.com/Y6Bzj

Tax Sales web site:

https://urlzs.com/2aB8X

Chapter 6

California Real Estate Investing City Goldmines

California Real Estate Investing
City Goldmines

1. Los Angeles

The city of Los Angeles has a population of 3,949,776 to support your real estate investing business.

The **median home value** in Los Angeles is $686,100. Los Angeles is a real estate goldmine city because recently the home values have gone up 2.2 percent and is expected to lower only -.1 percent.

Houses currently listed in Los Angeles have a median list price of about $829,994. Homes that actually sold have a median price of about $706,900.

The **median rent price** in Los Angeles is about $3,500 a month.

Foreclosure Warning sign

Delinquent mortgages in Los Angeles is .7 percent. The *Foreclosure potiential rank is #3 between California goldmine cities.*

California Real Estate Investing

City Goldmines

2. San Diego

The city of San Diego has a population of 1,390,966 to support your real estate investing business.

The **median home value** in San Diego is $633,600. San Diego is a real estate goldmine city because recently the home values have gone up 1.7 percent and is expected to rise at least another 0.2 percent.

Houses currently listed in San Diego have a median list price of about $705,000. Homes that actually sold have a median price of about $601,300.

The **median rent price** in San Diego is about $2,750 a month.

Foreclosure Warning sign

Delinquent mortgages in San Diego is .4 percent. The *Foreclosure potiential rank is #6 between California goldmine cities.*

California Real Estate Investing

City Goldmines

3. San Francisco

The city of San Francisco has a population of 864,263 to support your real estate investing business.

The median home value in San Francisco is $1,357,500. San Francisco is a real estate goldmine city because recently the home values have gone up 3.0 percent and is expected to fall only -.1 percent.

Houses currently listed in San Francisco have a median price of about $1,299,000.

The median rent price in San Francisco is about $4,506 a month.

Foreclosure Warning sign

Delinquent mortgages in San Francisco is .2 percent The *Foreclosure potiential rank is #7 the least among the California goldmine cities.*

California Real Estate Investing
City Goldmines

4. Fresno

The city of Fresno has a population of 519,037 to support your real estate investing business.

The median home value in Fresno is $242,500. Fresno is a real estate goldmine city because recently the home values have gone up 6.5 percent and is expected to rise at least another 3.6 percent.

Houses currently listed in Fresno have a median price of about $284,900. Homes that actually sold have a median list price of about $249,800.

The median rent price in Fresno is about $1,400 a month.

Foreclosure Warning sign

Delinquent mortgages in Fresno is 1.1 percent. The *Foreclosure potiential rank is #2 between California goldmine cities.*

California Real Estate Investing
City Goldmines

5. Sacramento

The city of Sacramento has a population of 489,650 to support your real estate investing business.

The median home value in Sacramento is $326,900. Sacramento is a real estate goldmine city because recently the home values have gone up 4.3 percent and is expected to rise at least another 1.9 percent.

Houses currently listed in Sacramento have a median price of about $330,000. Homes that actually sold have a median list price of about $315,100.

The median rent price in Sacramento is about $1,750 a month.

Foreclosure Warning sign

Delinquent mortgages in Sacramento is .7 percent. The *Foreclosure potiential rank is #3 between California goldmine cities.*

California Real Estate Investing
City Goldmines

6. Long Beach

The city of Long Beach has a population of 470,489 to support your real estate investing business.

The median home value in Long Beach is $593,500. Long Beach is a real estate goldmine city because recently the home values have gone up 2.0 percent and is expected to rise at least another .3 percent.

Houses currently listed in Long Beach have a median price of about $599,000. Homes that actually sold have a median list price of about $557,300.

The median rent price in Long Beach is about $2,300 a month.

Foreclosure Warning sign

Delinquent mortgages in Long Beach is .6 percent. The *Foreclosure potiential rank is #5 between California goldmine cities.*

California Real Estate Investing

City Goldmines

7. Bakersfield

The city of Bakersfield has a population of 372,680 to support your real estate investing business.

The median home value in Bakersfield is $241,600. Bakersfield is a real estate goldmine city because recently the home values have gone up 5.2 percent and is expected to rise at least another 2.6 percent.

Houses currently listed in Bakersfield have a median price of about $276,700. Homes that actually sold have a median list price of about $249,300.

The median rent price in Bakersfield is about $1,500 a month.

Foreclosure Warning sign

Delinquent mortgages in Bakersfield is 1.5 percent. Bakersfield has the greatest foreclosure *potiential of the California goldmine cities and is ranked #1 in that category.*

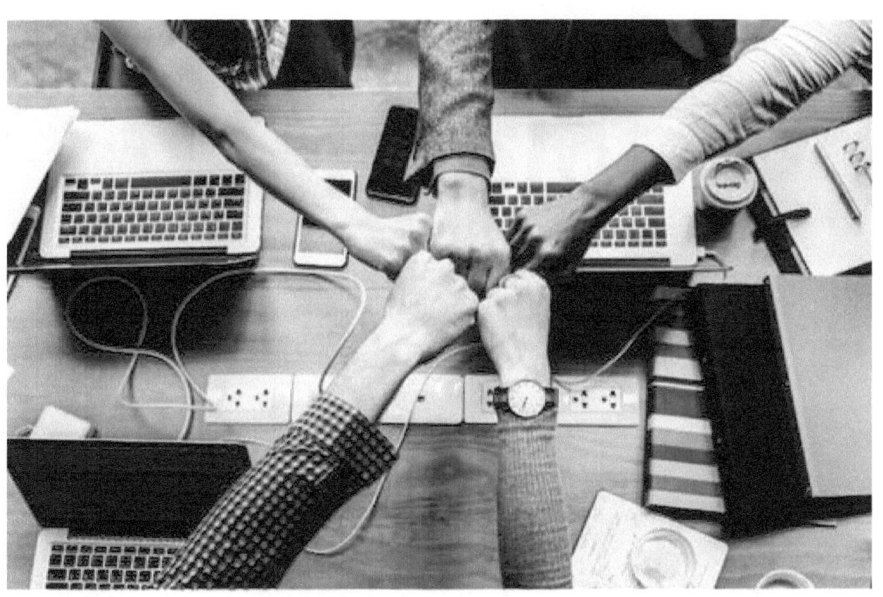

Chapter 7

Goldmine of Government Grants

How to write a Winning Grant Proposal

Goldmine of Government Grants

Government grants. Many people either don't believe government grants exist or they don't think they would ever be able to get government grant money.

First lets make one thing clear. Government grant money is **YOUR MONEY**. Government money comes from taxes paid by residents of this country. Depending on what state you live in, you are paying taxes on almost everything....Property tax for your house. Property tax on your car. Taxes on the things you purchase in the mall, or at the gas station. Taxes on your gasoline, the food you buy etc.

So get yourself in the frame of mind that you are not a charity case or too proud to ask for help, because billionaire companies like GM, Big Banks and most of Corporate America is not hesitating to get their share of **YOUR MONEY**!

There are over two thousand three hundred (2,300) Federal Government Assistance Programs. Some are loans but many are formula grants and project grants. To see all of the programs available go to:

https://beta.sam.gov/help/assistance-listing

WRITING A GRANT PROPOSAL

The Basic Components of a Proposal

There are eight basic components to creating a solid proposal package:

1. The proposal summary;

2. Introduction of organization;

3. The problem statement   (or needs assessment);

4. Project objectives;

5. Project methods or design;

6. Project evaluation;

7. Future funding; and

8. The project budget.

WRITING A GRANT PROPOSAL

The Proposal Summary

The Proposal Summary is an outline of the project goals and objectives. Keep the Proposal Summary short and to the point. No more that 2 or 3 paragraphs. Put it at the beginning of the proposal.

Introduction

The Introduction portion of your grant proposal presents you and your business as a credible applicant and organization.

Highlight the accomplishments of your organization from all sources: newspaper or online articles etc. Include a biography of key members and leaders. State the goals and philosophy of the company.

The Problem Statement

The problem statement makes clear the problem you are going to solve(maybe reduce homelessness). Make sure to use facts. State who and how those affected will benefit from solving the problem. State the exact manner in how you will solve the problem.

WRITING A GRANT PROPOSAL

Project Objectives

The Project Objectives section of your grant proposal focuses on the Goals and Desired outcome.

Make sure to indentify all objectives and how you are going to reach these objectives. The more statistics you can find to support your objectives the better. Make sure to put in realistic objectives. You may be judged on how well you accomplish what you said you intended to do.

Program Methods and Design

The program methods and design section of your grant proposal is a detailed plan of action.

>What resources are going to be used.

>What staff is going to be needed.

>System development.

>Create a Flow Chart of project features.

>Explain what will be achieved.

>Try to produce evidence of what will be achieved.

>Make a diagram of program design.

WRITING A GRANT PROPOSAL

Evaluation

There is product evaluation and process evaluation. The product evaluation deals with the result that relate to the project and how well the project has met it's objectives.

The process evaluation deals with how the project was conducted, how did it line up with the original stated plan and the overall effectiveness of the different aspects of the plan.

Evaluations can start at anytime during the project or at the project's conclusion. It is advised to submit a evaluation design at the start of a project.

It looks better if you have collected convincing data before and during the program.

If evaluation design is not presented at the beginning that might encourage a critical review of the program design.

Future Funding

The Future Funding part of the grant proposal should have long term project planning past the grant period.

WRITING A GRANT PROPOSAL

Budget

Utilities, rental equipment, staffing, salary, food, transportation, phone bills and insurance are just some of the things to include in the budget.

A well constructed budget accounts for every penny.

For a complete guide for government grants google

catalog of federal domestic assistance. You can download a complete PDF version of the catalog.

Other sources of Government Funding

You can get General Small Business loans from the government. Go to the Small Business Administration for more information.

SBA Microloan Program

The Microloan program provides loans of up to $50,000 with the average loan being $13,000.

https://www.sba.gov/

Here are a Few Current Commercial Real Estate Grant/Loan Programs

Program Number: 10.415

Program Name: Rural Rental Housing Loans

Department: Department of Agriculture

Assistance: Grants - Direct Loans

Program Number: 10.438

Program Name: Section 538 Rural Rental

Department: Department of Agriculture

Assistance: Guaranteed Loans

Program Number: 14.191

Program Name: Multifamily Housing

Department: HUD

Assistance: Project Grants

A Few Current Commercial Real Estate Grant/Loan Programs

Program Number: 14.314

Program Name: Assisted Living Conversion

Department: HUD

Assistance: Project Grants

Program Number: 14.326

Program Name: Rental Assistance 811

Department: HUD

Assistance: Project Grants

Program Number: 14.329

Program Name: HUD Multifamily PSF Pilot

Department: HUD

Assistance: Direct Payments for Specified Use

WRITING A GRANT PROPOSAL

Recently billionaire Elon Musk was awarded 4.9 billion dollars in government subsidies. If you are hesitant to pursue government assistance, let that sink in. A billionaire who pays little in taxes was given billions of your tax dollars.

Government grants are real. Like anything else worthwhile, there is effort and qualifications that must be met to obtain them.

Chapter 8
Business Insurance

BUSINESS INSURANCE

Consult an attorney for any and all of your business matters.

In the early 1990's an elderly woman purchased a hot cup of coffee from a McDonald's drive-thru window in Albuquerque. She spilled the coffee, and suffered 3rd degree burns. She sued Mcdonald's and won. She won 2.7 million dollars in a punitive damages victory. The verdict was appealed and settlement is estimated at somewhere in the neighborhood of $500,000 dollars. All because she spilled the coffee into her lap, while trying to add sugar and cream.

Two men in Ohio, were carpet layers. They were severely burned when a three and a half gallon container of carpet adhesive ignited, when the hot water heater it was sitting next to, was turned on. They felt the warning lable on the back of the can was insufficient. So they filed a lawsuit against the adhesive manufacturers and were awarded nine million dollars.

A woman in Oklahoma, purchased a brand new Winnebago. While driving it home, she set the cruise control to 70 miles per hour. She then left the drivers seat to make some coffee or a sandwich in the back of the motor home.

BUSINESS INSURANCE

The vehicle crashed and the woman sued Winnebago for not advising her, that cruise control does not drive and steer the vehicle. She won 1.7 million dollars and the company had to rewrite their instruction manual.

Unfortunately all three outrageous lawsuits are real. If you are going to run a business, any business, you should consider protecting yourself with Professional Liability Insurance, also known as Errors and Omissions (E & O) insurance.

This type of insurance can help to protect you from having to pay the full cost of defending yourself against a negligence lawsuit claim.

Error and Omissions can protect you against claims that are not usually covered in regular liability insurance. Those policies usually cover bodily harm, or damage to property. Error and Omissions can protect you agaist negligence, and other mental anguish like inaccurate advice, or misrepresentation. Criminal prosecution is not covered.

Errors and Ommision insurance is recommended for notaries public, real estate brokers or investors and professionals like: software engineers, lawyers, home inspectors web site delvelopers and landscape architects to name a few professions.

BUSINESS INSURANCE

The Most Common Errors and Omission Claims:

%25 Breach of Fiduciary Duty

%15 Breach of Contract

%14 Negligence

%13 Failure to Supervise

%11 Unsuitability

%10 Other

BUSINESS INSURANCE

Things you should know about or require before purchasing a Errors and Omission policy is...

* What is the limit of liability

* What is the Deductible

* Does it include FDD First Dollar Defense - which obligates the insurance company to fight a case without a deductible first.

* Do I have Tail-end coverage or Extended Reporting Coverage (insurance that lasts into retirement)

* Extended coverage for Employees

* Cyber Liability Coverage

* Department of Labor Fiduciary Coverage

* Insolvency Coverage

If you get Errors and Omission insurance, renew it the day it expires. You must be careful to avoid gaps in your coverage, or it could result in not getting your policy renewed.

BUSINESS INSURANCE

A few E & O Insurance Providers:

Insureon

Insureon states that their median Errors and Omissions Insurance policy cost about $750 a year or about $65 a month. The price of course will vary according to your business, the policy you choose and other risk factors.

https://www.insureon.com/home

EOforless

EOforless.com helps insurance, investment, and real estate professionals buy E & O insurance at an affordable cost in five minutes or less.

https://www.eoforless.com/

BUSINESS INSURANCE

CalSurance Associates

As a leading insurance broker, CalSurance Associates, a division of Brown & Brown Program Insurance Services, Inc. has over fifty years of experience delivering comprehensive insurance products, exceptional service, and proven results to over 150,000 insured. They provide professionals nationwide and across multiple industries, including some of the largest financial firms and insurance companies in the United States.

http://www.calsurance.com/csweb/index.aspx

Better Safe Than Sorry

Insurance is one of the hidden costs of doing business. These are just a few companies and a brief overview on the topic of business insurance. Make sure to talk to an attorney or quailified insurance agent before making any decision on insurance. Protect you and your business. Many states do not require E & O insurances. But when you see the cost of some of the settlements, it's better to be safe than sorry.

Chapter 9

Millionaire Real Estate Investing Rolodex

Get Started Fast with these Business Web Sites

MILLIONAIRE ROLODEX

As of the writing of this book, all of the companies web site's are up and running. From time to time companies go out of business or change their web address. So, instead of just giving you just 1 source I give you plenty of sources to choose from.

Top 15 Most Popular eBizMBA Rank

Real Estate Websites

with Estimated Unique Monthly Visitors

1. **Zillow** — 36,000,000

2. **Trulia** — 23,000,000

3. **Yahoo! Homes** — 20,000,000

4. **Realtor** — 18,000,000

5. **Redfin** — 6,000,000

6. **Homes** — 5,000,000

MILLIONAIRE ROLODEX

Top 15 Most Popular eBizMBA Rank

Real Estate Websites	Monthly Visitors
7. **ApartmentGuide**	2,500,000
8. **Curbed**	2,000,000
9. **ReMax**	1,800,000
10. **HotPads**	1,750,000
11. **ZipRealty**	1,600,000
12. **Apartments**	1,500,000
13. **Rent**	1,400,000
14. **Auction**	1,300,000
15. **ForRent**	1,200,000

MILLIONAIRE ROLODEX

Nationwide Banks & Foreclosure Properties

Bank of America

http://foreclosures.bankofamerica.com/

Wells Fargo

https://reo.wellsfargo.com/

Ocwen Financial Corporation

http://www.ocwen.com/reo

Hubzu

http://www.hubzu.com/

MILLIONAIRE ROLODEX

Government Foreclosure Properties

Fannie Mae
The Federal National Mortgage Association

https://www.fanniemae.com/singlefamily/reo-vendors

Department of Housing and Urban Development

https://www.hudhomestore.com/Home/Index.aspx

The Federal Deposit Insurance Corporation

https://www.fdic.gov/buying/owned/

The **United States Department of Agriculture**

https://properties.sc.egov.usda.gov/resales/index.jsp

United States Marshals

https://www.usmarshals.gov/assets/sales.htm#real_estate

MILLIONAIRE ROLODEX

Commercial Real Estate Properties

City Feet

http://www.cityfeet.com/#

The Commercial Real Estate Listing Service

https://www.cimls.com/

Land . Net

http://www.land.net/

Loop . Net

http://www.loopnet.com/

MILLIONAIRE ROLODEX

FSBO – For Sale By Owner Properties

By Owner

http://www.byowner.com/

For sale by owner in Canada

http://www.fsbo-bc.com/

For sale by owner Central

http://www.fsbocentral.com/

For sale by Owner: world's largest FSBO web site

http://www.forsalebyowner.com/

Ranch by owner

http://www.ranchbyowner.com/

MILLIONAIRE ROLODEX

Tools to Get You Started Video Marketing

https://www.YouTube.com/

Upload your videos to this web site.

https://www.wikipedia.org/

Get valuable information for video topics.

https://screencast-o-matic.com/

Use this screen capture software to create videos

http://www.openoffice.org/download/

Use this Open source word processor software to make slides for your videos.

MILLIONAIRE ROLODEX

Free Keyword Tools

Google keyword planner

https://adwords.google.com/home/tools/keyword-planner/

SEO Centro

http://www.seocentro.com/

Ubersuggest

https://ubersuggest.io/

Promoting Your Real Estate/Videos

Top Free Press Release Websites

https://www.prlog.org

https://www.pr.com

https://www.pr-inside.com

https://www.newswire.com

https://www.OnlinePRNews.com

MILLIONAIRE ROLODEX

Top Social Media Websites

https://www.facebook.com

https://www.tumbler.com

https://www.pinterest.com

https://www.reddit.com

https://www.linkedin.com/

http://digg.com/

https://twitter.com

https://instagram.com

For Everything Under the Sun at Wholesale Prices

http://www.liquidation.com/

COMPUTERS/Office Equipment

http://www.wtsmedia.com/

http://www.laptopplaza.com/

http://www.outletpc.com/

MILLIONAIRE ROLODEX

With this "Millionaire Rolodex" of real estate business resources, you have a ton of web sites that you can use to get started working on your real estate business with little to no money.

So take advantage of these resources to continue to gain valuable knowledge, save money and promote your real estate business.

Chapter 10

REAL ESTATE INVESTING TERMS

REAL ESTATE TERMS

Accrued Interest - In finance, accrued interest is the interest on a bond or loan that has accumulated since the principal investment, or since the previous coupon payment if there has been one already. For a financial instrument such as a bond, interest is calculated and paid in set intervals (for instance annually or semi-annually).

Adjustable Rate Mortgage (ARM) - A variable-rate mortgage, adjustable-rate mortgage (ARM), or tracker mortgage is a mortgage loan with the interest rate on the note periodically adjusted based on an index which reflects the cost to the lender of borrowing on the credit markets.

Alienation clause - A clause in a mortgage contract that requires full payment of the balance of a mortgage at the lender's discretion if the property is sold or the title to the property changes to another person. Nearly all mortgages have an alienation clause.

Amortization - Amortization is an accounting term that refers to the process of allocating the cost of an intangible asset over a period of time. It also refers to the repayment of loan principal over time.

REAL ESTATE TERMS

Appraised value - An appraised value is an evaluation of a property's value based on a given point in time that is performed by a professional appraiser during the mortgage origination process. The appraiser is usually chosen by the lender, but the appraisal is paid for by the borrower.

Arbitration clause - An arbitration clause is a clause in a contract that requires the parties to resolve their disputes through an arbitration process

Assignee - a person to whom a right or liability is legally transferred.

Assumption of mortgage - Mortgage assumption is the conveyance of the terms and balance of an existing mortgage to the purchaser of a financed property, commonly requiring that the assuming party is qualified under lender or guarantor guidelines.

Backup offer - A backup offer is when a home seller has accepted an offer from a buyer, but is still accepting offers from other buyers. Sellers state that they are accepting backup offers if they think the current offer may fall through.

REAL ESTATE TERMS

Binder insurance - binder. A legal agreement issued by either an agent or an insurer to provide temporary evidence of insurance until a policy can be issued. Binders should contain definite time limits, should be in writing, and should clearly designate the insurer with which the risk is bound

Cash basis taxpayer - A taxpayer who reports income and deductions in the year that they are actually paid or received. Cash basis taxpayers cannot report receivables as income, nor deduct promissory notes as payments.

Certificate of title - A certificate of title is a state or municipal-issued document that identifies the owner or owners of personal or real property. A certificate of title provides documentary evidence of the right of ownership.

Cloud on title - Any document, claim, unreleased lien or encumbrance that might invalidate or impair the title to real property or make the title doubtful. Clouds on title are usually discovered during a title search. Clouds on title are resolved through initiating a quitclaim deed or a commencement of action to quiet title.

REAL ESTATE TERMS

Commission - A fee charged by a broker or agent for his/her service in facilitating a transaction, such as the buying or selling of securities or real estate. In the case of securities trading, brokers can be split into two broad categories depending on the commissions they charge.

Debt coverage ratio - In corporate finance, DSCR refers to the amount of cash flow available to meet annual interest and principal payments on debt, including sinking fund payments. In personal finance, DSCR refers to a ratio used by bank loan officers in determining debt servicing ability.

Deed of trust - In real estate in the United States, a deed of trust or trust deed is a deed wherein legal title in real property is transferred to a trustee, which holds it as security for a loan (debt) between a borrower and lender. The equitable title remains with the borrower.

Due diligence - Due diligence means taking caution, performing calculations, reviewing documents, procuring insurance, walking the property, etc. — essentially doing your homework for the property BEFORE you actually make the purchase

REAL ESTATE TERMS

Encroachment - A situation in real estate where a property owner violates the property rights of his neighbor by building something on the neighbor's land or by allowing something to hang over onto the neighbor's property.

Escrow instructions - n. the written instructions by buyer and seller of real estate given to a title company, escrow company or individual escrow in "closing" a real estate transaction. These instructions are generally prepared by the escrow holder and then approved by the parties and their agents. (See: closing, escrow)

Fair market value - The fair market value is the price at which the property would change hands between a willing buyer and a willing seller, neither being under any compulsion to buy or to sell and both having reasonable knowledge of relevant facts.

Foreclosure - Foreclosure is a legal process in which a lender attempts to recover the balance of a loan from a borrower, who has stopped making payments to the lender, by forcing the sale of the asset used as the collateral for the loan.

REAL ESTATE TERMS

Grantor - First, it's important to review the legal definition of "grantor" and "grantee." In a real estate transaction, the grantor is the party that conveys the property in question. The grantor may be an individual, business entity or partnership. The grantee is the party that receives the property

Highest and best use - The Appraisal Institute defines highest and best use as follows: The reasonably probable and legal use of vacant land or an improved property that is physically possible, appropriately supported, financially feasible, and that results in the highest value.

Insurable title - Marketable Title vs. Insurable Title. ... When a title is marketable it means that the chain of ownership (title) to a particular piece of property is clear and free from defects. And as such, it can be marketed for sale without additional effort by the seller or potential buyer.

Involuntary lien - involuntary lien. A lien on real estate that results without the property owners' voluntary cooperation in the placement of the lien. Examples include tax liens and judgment liens. Contrast with a mortgage, which is voluntary.

REAL ESTATE TERMS

Judgment proof - People are judgment-proof if they lack the resources or insurance to pay a court judgment against them. For example, suppose that a thief steals your car, sells it, and then burns all of his worldly possessions. Even if you sued him and won, you could not recover anything because the thief is judgment-proof.

Leverage - Leverage is the use of various financial instruments or borrowed capital to increase the potential return of an investment – and it is an extremely common term on both Wall Street and in the Main Street real estate market. (Learn more about the various uses of leverage in Leveraged Investment Showdown.)

Lis pendens - In United States law, a lis pendens is a written notice that a lawsuit has been filed concerning real estate, involving either the title to the property or a claimed ownership interest in it.

Mechanics lien - A guarantee of payment to builders, contractors and construction firms that build or repair structures. Mechanic's liens also extend to suppliers of materials and subcontractors and cover building repairs as well.

REAL ESTATE TERMS

Net income - Net operating income (NOI) is a calculation used to analyze real estate investments that generate income. Net operating income equals all revenue from the property minus all reasonably necessary operating expenses

Obsolescence - Functional obsolescence is a reduction in the usefulness or desirability of an object because of an outdated design feature, usually one that cannot be easily changed. The term is commonly used in real estate, but has a wide application.

Point - In real estate mortgages, a point refers to the origination fee charged by the lender, with each point being equal to 1% of the amount of the loan. It can also refer to each percentage difference between a mortgage's interest rate and the prime interest rate.

Preliminary title report - A preliminary title sets forth various details about a piece of real estate, including: Ownership; Liens and encumbrances; and Easements. The information in a preliminary title report, also known as a title search, is gathered from the property records in the county where the property is located.

REAL ESTATE TERMS

Pro forma - What does 'Pro Forma' mean. Pro forma, a Latin term, literally means "for the sake of form" or "as a matter of form." In the world of investing, pro forma refers to a method by which financial results are calculated. This method of calculation places emphasis on present or projected figures.

Quit claim deed - A quitclaim deed is a legal instrument which is used to transfer interest in real property. The entity transferring its interest is called the grantor, and when the quitclaim deed is properly completed and executed, it transfers any interest the grantor has in the property to a recipient, called the grantee.

Realized gain - The amount by which the sale price of an asset exceeds its purchase price. Unless the realized gain came from a tax-exempt or tax-deferred asset, it is taxable. However, the type of taxation to which it is subject varies according to how long the asset has been owned. A realized gain from an asset owned longer than one year is usually taxed at the capital gains rate, while an asset owned for a period shorter than a year is often subject to the higher income tax rate. It is also called the recognized gain.

REAL ESTATE TERMS

Replacement cost - A replacement cost is the cost to replace an asset of a company at the same or equal value, and the asset to be replaced could be a building, investment securities, accounts receivable or liens.

Restrictive covenant - A restrictive covenant is any type of agreement that requires the buyer to either take or abstain from a specific action. In real estate transactions, restrictive covenants are binding legal obligations written into the deed of a property by the seller.

Short-rate - The relatively higher insurance premium rate charged for coverage when one cancels a policy earlier than originally agreed upon. Rather than receiving a pro rata refund of the unearned premium, the property owner receives a smaller amount.

Subordination - For an individual, the most frequent example of a subordination agreement is when an individual attempts to refinance the first mortgage on a property which has a second mortgage. The second mortgage has a lower priority than the first mortgage, but these priorities may be upset by refinancing the loan.

REAL ESTATE TERMS

Tax shelter -Tax shelters can range from investments or investment accounts that provide favorable tax ... evasion, the illegal avoidance of taxes through misrepresentation or similar means. ... A tax shelter product designed to create large, seemingly real .

Title - a right or claim to the ownership of property or to a rank or throne.

Usury - the illegal action or practice of lending money at unreasonably high rates of interest.

Warranty deed - a deed that guarantees a clear title to the buyer of real property.

Wrap-around - "wrap", is a form of secondary financing for the purchase of real property. The seller extends to the buyer a junior mortgage which wraps around and exists in addition to any superior mortgages already secured by the property.

Join Our VIP Mailing List! Get FREE Money Making Training Videos! Then Start Making Money within 24 hours!
Plus when you join our Mailing list you can get Free bonus coupons for all our new ACX Audible Audio Books!

But don't wait, ACX only gives us a limited supply of free audio book coupons, so join right now!

Just use the following link...

https://mahoneyproducts.wixsite.com/win1

MegaSized Marketing

How to get a million dollars worth of advertising Free!

142 complete training videos!

YouTube Video Marketing
How to Build a Customer Email List.
Email Marketing
Expert Copy writing
How to set up a Squeeze page
How to get Massive Traffic to your web site or videos!
Quick and easy step by step training!
Just go to…
https://ebay.to/2JF08nY

Please Leave a Review!

There is not another real estate investing book on the market that gives you as many sources for wholesale real estate than this book.

My book gives you more and in most cases for less!

This book also gives you a web site that has over 4,000 sources of real estate financing in addition to the government's over 2,400 sources of Federal Assistance.

I have enjoyed doing all the research and sharing my real world real estate investing experience in what I hope is easy to understand terminology.

So I ask you to leave a honest and hopefully great review!

Thank you.

Warm Regards,

www.ingramcontent.com/pod-product-compliance
Lightning Source LLC
Chambersburg PA
CBHW021833170526
45157CB00007B/2790